Stephen Curry

The Inspirational Story of Basketball Superstar Stephen Curry

Copyright 2015 by Bill Redban - All rights reserved.

This document is geared towards providing exact and reliable information in regards to the topic and issue covered. The publication is sold with the idea that the publisher is not required to render accounting, officially permitted, or otherwise qualified services. If advice is necessary, legal or professional, a practiced individual in the profession should be ordered.

In no way is it legal to reproduce, duplicate, or transmit any part of this document in either electronic means or printed format. Recording of this publication is strictly prohibited and any storage of this document is not allowed unless with written permission from the publisher. All rights reserved.

The information provided herein is stated to be truthful and consistent, in that any liability, in terms of inattention or otherwise, by any usage or abuse of any policies, processes, or directions contained within is the solitary and utter responsibility of the recipient reader. Under no circumstances will any legal responsibility or blame be held against the publisher for any reparation, damages, or monetary loss due to the information herein, either directly or indirectly.

The information herein is offered for informational purposes solely, and is universal as so. The presentation of the information is without contract or any type of guarantee assurance.

The trademarks that are used are without any consent, and the publication of the trademark is without permission or backing by the trademark owner. All trademarks and brands within this book are for clarifying purposes only and are owned by the owners themselves, not affiliated with this document.

Table Of Contents

Introduction

As the title already implies, this is a short book about [The Inspirational Story of Basketball Superstar Stephen Curry] and how he rose from his life in North Carolina to becoming one of today's leading and most respected basketball players. In his rise to superstardom, Stephen has inspired not only the youth, but fans of all ages, throughout the world.

This book also portrays the struggles that Stephen has had to overcome during his early childhood years, his teen years, and up until he became what he is today. A notable source of inspiration is Stephen's consistent support of charitable organizations, such as the Boys and Girls Foundation, along with numerous others. Combining incredible accuracy, intelligent decision-making, quick feet, and superior coordination, Stephen has shown the ability to slice up any kind of defense. He continues to serve as the humble, mild-mannered superstar

in a sport that glorifies flashy plays and mega personalities.

Thanks again for grabbing this book. Hopefully you can take some of the examples from Stephen's story and apply them to your own life!

Chapter 1:

Early Childhood/Family Life

Stephen "Steph" Curry was born on March 14th, 1988 in Akron, Ohio. He is legally named Wardell Stephen Curry II, after his grandfather Wardell "Jack" Curry, and his father Wardell Stephen "Dell" Curry I. Stephen's grandmother was named Juanita but everyone affectionately called her Duckie.

Stephen was raised in a family of athletes. His father was one of the most formidable sharpshooters in the NBA during the 1990s. Nowadays, he plies his wares as a broadcaster for the Charlotte Hornets franchise. Dell started garnering attention while playing for Fort Defiance High School in Virginia. His coach remembers allowing Dell to shoot hoops at his barn. This is where Dell honed his skills as a basketball player, particularly as a sharpshooter.

Dell graduated from Fort Defiance as its all-time leader in points scored. He was also named to the prestigious McDonald's High School All-American team in 1992. He later starred for the Virginia Tech Hokies, where he earned numerous accolades such as the Metro Conference Player of the Year and Consensus All-American Second Team honors.

Dell started playing in the NBA in 1986. He was selected as the 15th overall pick by the Utah Jazz. He also played for the Cleveland Cavaliers, Milwaukee Bucks, Toronto Raptors, and the Charlotte Hornets in a 16-year career. Dell retired in 2002 as the Charlotte Hornets all-time leader in points scored and three-point field goals made. He was also named the NBA Sixth Man of the Year in 1994.

Growing up, Dell was a two-sport star. Aside from basketball, he was a skilled baseball player. As a matter of fact, he was twice drafted by

Major League Baseball franchises - the Texas Rangers who drafted him in 1982 out of high school, and the Baltimore Orioles who drafted him in the 14th round of the 1985 draft.

Stephen's mother, Sonya Adams-Curry, was a basketball and volleyball star during her high school years at Radford High. She won state championships in both sports during this time period. Sonya then matriculated at Virginia Tech, where she also played for the basketball and volleyball varsity teams. Sonya was considered a volleyball star during her college years.

Having Dell and Sonya as parents obviously gave Stephen a top-notch athletic pedigree, which he also shares with his two siblings.

Stephen is the eldest of the Curry brood. His younger brother, Seth, is a basketball player as well. He played at Liberty College for a year, before transferring to Duke University where he finished his collegiate career. Seth averaged 17.5 points in his final year with the Duke Blue Devils. He was part of the 2013 All-ACC First Team and was named a Second Team All-American by *The Sporting News*.

Seth also played for the gold medal-winning United States men's basketball team in the 2009 U-19 World Championship, held in New Zealand. But in the cut-throat world of professional basketball, all those achievements weren't enough to guarantee his place in the NBA. After he went undrafted in the 2013 NBA Draft, Seth received an invite to train with the Golden State Warriors during that year's preseason. However, he wasn't able to make the final roster for opening night.

Seth spent the first years of his professional career playing in the NBA Developmental League. There, he was named to the 2014 All-Rookie First Team, All-NBA D-League First and Third Team and twice played in the All-Star Game. Seth made his NBA debut for Memphis after he was signed by the Grizzlies. Unfortunately, he was quickly waived after playing one game and registering zero statistics save for four minutes of playing time.

Seth bounced back and forth from the NBA to the D-League since. In between his stint with the D-League's Santa Cruz Warriors and Erie BayHawks, Seth signed a ten-day contract with the Cleveland Cavaliers, and played for the

Orlando Magic, Phoenix Suns, and New Orleans Pelicans' Summer League teams. He was finally signed to a full contract by the Sacramento Kings in 2015.

Stephen's younger sister, Sydel, is a volleyball player just like their mother. She is currently a freshman, playing for the Elon University Volleyball Team as a setter. Sydel was considered one of the premier high school athletes in her sport. She was supposed to play her first game in 2014. Unfortunately she suffered an injury during preseason practice and was forced to redshirt. Upon her return to the volleyball court in 2015, Sydel proved she is still one of the players to watch out for. In fact, she was named captain of the Elon University Volleyball Team.

After spending a year each with the Jazz and the Cavaliers, Dell Curry was placed in the expansion pool where he was picked up by then newcomer, Charlotte Hornets. Dell would spend the best years of his basketball career with the Hornets, where he would become one of its most popular players. The Curry family transferred to Charlotte full-time. This is where Stephen Curry's first taste of organized basketball began.

While Dell was busy burying threes in the NBA, Sonya started the Christian Montessori School in Lake Norman, North Carolina. The family was supportive of Sonya's endeavor. As a matter of fact, Stephen's grandmother and aunt also worked in the school as cook and teacher, respectively. Not only that, Stephen and his siblings studied there during their early years. Later, the family moved to Canada on account of Dell being traded to the Toronto Raptors. Dell spent three years, from 1999 to 2002, as a Raptor before calling it quits from professional basketball.

Stephen spent 7th and 8th grade playing basketball for Queensway Christian College in Etobicoke, Ontario. While with the school, the varsity team went undefeated in one season.

Stephen and Seth used to attend their father's practices. Sometimes they'd just sit back and watch. Other times they'd clown around with the players. Most of the time, they worked on their own skill-set. Stephen was already a gym rat at that young age. He would be in the Air Canada Centre practicing his stroke before the Raptors started their practice session.

He was also one of the last ones to leave. Stephen played one-on-one games with some of his dad's teammates including Muggsy Bogues, Vince Carter, Tracy McGrady, and even Mark Jackson. Alvin Williams, the starting point guard for the Raptors at the time, remembers playing against the young Curry. The then 5-foot Stephen went against the 6'5" Williams who never gave the youngster a breather. Or was it the other way around?

"I had to guard him seriously," Williams recalled. "He could fire from deep and it was consistent." Williams played real defense on the young shooter. The now-retired NBA guard knew that if he let Stephen reach nine points, he could potentially lose the game.

Stephen wouldn't be this good if it weren't for his father and to a certain extent, his Grandpa Jack. Thanks in part to the influence of his father, young Stephen learned about the game of basketball at a very young age. Dell himself, got into the game early in life. Stephen's father lived in Grottoes, Virginia with his family as a youngster in the 1970s.

Dell's father, Jack, was worried that his young son would get into trouble if he played outdoors - particularly in the woods where bears were known to roam. In addition to that, Dell had four sisters playing with their dolls, so he didn't have much to do inside the house. Jack needed to figure out how to keep young Dell preoccupied during the summer break.

So, he set up a hoop outside their home where Dell would later discover his love for the sport of basketball. Jack used an old utility pole, an unpredictable fiberglass backboard and some fabricated steel brackets to make the hoop. Dell played every chance he got and slowly honed his skills. Years later, he would see the same perseverance in his children.

Stephen and Seth used to duke it out every time they visited their grandma in Grottoes. The Curry boys, including Dell, would challenge each other to see who could hit a 60 foot shot. During normal shoot-arounds, they had to make the shot if they didn't want the hassle of chasing the ball whenever they'd miss. According to Stephen, it was "make it or chase it". Grandpa Jack, unfortunately, didn't live long enough to see his grandsons use the hoop he built along his gravel driveway for their father. But that was a catalyst in why the boys fell in love with basketball - particularly the three point shot.

Chapter 2:

High School Career

Despite having athletic DNA passed down from his parents, Stephen has always looked like one of those unassuming athletes. His advantages, even in the NBA, have never really been his jumping ability or speed. In fact, in his senior year of high school, Stephen barely measured at 6'0" and weighed just below 160 pounds, which is considerably small in the cut-throat world of collegiate basketball.

For high school, Stephen enrolled at Charlotte Christian School in Charlotte, North Carolina, where he would show flashes of potential almost immediately. His high school coach, Shonn Brown, remembers having a problem with Stephen's basketball uniform because of his diminutive frame. While his teammates' uniform sizes were mostly large, Stephen's was medium. And that's only because they couldn't order the small size.

When Stephen played, you could see that his jersey and shorts were loose. The future superstar joked about his frame and talked about needing to "fill this thing (uniform) out." Essentially, he wanted to bulk up a bit so his uniform wouldn't bounce around while he ran. Despite his size (or lack of), it was evident early-on that this young man had a very uncanny ability to knock in difficult shots - with amazing range.

But there was actually a time that he had to be told to shoot more often. During his sophomore year, the then 5'8" reed-thin Curry was more of a pass-first guard. But things changed for the better the following year, after his coach sat him down and talked to him about his potential as a scorer. Coach Brown told Stephen to take advantage of his shooting ability a little more.

With his shooting prowess and impressive playmaking ability, Stephen led the Charlotte Christian Knights to three conference championships and 3 state playoff appearances. During his senior year, the school went 33-3 and people started to notice them. During the Chick-fil-A Classic, the Knights went head-to-head with the likes of St. Anthony (New Jersey) and Norcross (Georgia), two powerhouse high schools.

St. Anthony produced the likes of former NBA players David Rivers, Bobby Hurley, Terry Dehere, Rodrick Rhodes, Roshown McLeod, and current San Antonio Spur Kyle Anderson. Norcross, meanwhile, counts Jodie Meeks, Gani Lawal, Al-Farouq Aminu, and Jeremy Lamb among their notable alumni. Meeks and Lawal were the stars of Norcross when they played the Knights during the tournament. Stephen put on a show as his team upset the favored Norcross Blue Devils.

More than just enjoying team success, Stephen enjoyed individual success as well. Not only was he an all-conference MVP, but he also became an all-state MVP, boosting his status as perhaps the best high school baller in North Carolina.

Despite all the accolades he received, and having the "Curry" name, Stephen was never heavily recruited out of high school. He was only rated as a three-star recruit by *Scout* and *Rivals*. Overall, he was the 245th player and 51st best point guard coming out of high school, according to a consensus ranking of the top recruiting services. None of the major Division-1 schools offered him a scholarship.

His dream school, Virginia Tech (where his father Dell starred from 1983-1986), offered him a slot on the team, but only as a walk-on. In the end, only 3 schools offered Stephen a scholarship, with all of them being Division 1 schools that belonged to mid-major conferences: Davidson, Virginia Commonwealth, and Winthrop. Stephen ended up choosing Davidson. His new school was an afterthought in the college basketball scene, even if it was a Division-1 team. Before Stephen showed up, the last time Davidson had won a game in the NCAA Tournament was in 1969.

Despite being offered a full-ride athletic scholarship to play basketball collegiately, it was very difficult for Stephen to stomach the fact that he was not wanted by the top schools in the country. This was especially hard considering he was easily one of the top, if not the best, basketball players in the state of North Carolina.

Once again, Stephen knew that he had to work hard to prove himself; this was where his character would be tested. He had two choices - give up on the dream of playing basketball in the NBA, or prove the doubters wrong and work his butt   off.

Chapter 3:

College Period

While Stephen was not recruited heavily out of high school, Davidson Wildcats coach Bob McKillop envisioned big things for him. To quote him, McKillop said at a Davidson alumni event, "Wait 'til you see Stephen Curry. He is something special."

McKillop sure sounded prophetic, as Stephen Curry started his freshman year on fire. His first game against Eastern Michigan was a contradiction of sorts. He scored 15 points - which was good for any freshman player. However, he also committed 13 turnovers due to first game jitters. Stephen bounced back big-time in Davidson's next game, where he scored 32 points against the college basketball powerhouse Michigan Wolverines. Stephen added four assists and nine rebounds in the game.

As a freshman, Stephen led the entire Southern Conference in scoring, averaging 21.5 points per game. This same scoring clip was the second-highest in the nation among freshmen, only behind Kevin Durant, who was playing for the University of Texas. Stephen also set a new NCAA freshman record for most 3-pointers made in a season, with 113, further cementing his claim on the conference's Freshman of the Year award. He was also named SoCon Tournament MVP and was included in the All-Tournament team and All-SoCon First Team.

But, perhaps most importantly, Stephen helped lead Davidson to a 29-5 record for the season, win the Southern Conference championship, and earn a slot in the NCAA Tournament. While Davidson lost in the first round of the NCAA Tournament against Maryland, they earned the respect of fans around the nation - with a valiant performance, most notably from Stephen, who scored 30 points in that game.

After his freshman season, Stephen was chosen to be part of the Men's Basketball Team that represented the United Sates in the FIBA Under-19 World Championship - held in Novi Sad, Serbia. The team, which was coached by Jerry Wainwright, and featured other college stars and future NBA players such as Michael Beasley, DeAndre Jordan, Patrick Beverley, Donté Greene and Jonny Flynn, failed to live up to expectations. The team lost to a determined Serbian team led by tournament MVP Milan Mačvan during the championship game. However, Stephen played an important role on the team, as he averaged 9.4 points and 2.2 assists in just under 20 minutes of playing time per game.

Due to their impressive performances during the previous season, expectations for the future were high at Davidson University. During his sophomore season, the now 6'3" Stephen averaged 25.9 points per game to lead the Wildcats and the Southern Conference. Davidson finished with a 26-6 record (in spite of a tougher non-conference schedule) and went undefeated in the Southern Conference.

Once again, they earned a slot in the NCAA Tournament. This time, they went further, knocking out Gonzaga, Georgetown, and Wisconsin in succession. In the game against the Gonzaga Bulldogs, Davidson was down by 11 points early, but a 30-point splurge by Stephen, who finished with 40, propelled them into the next round. The eighth-seeded Georgetown Hoyas were expected to reach the Final Four, but Stephen and the Wildcats would not have any of that. Stephen exploded in the second half to lead his team over the Hoyas, 74-70.

Stephen dropped 33 points on the Wisconsin Badgers in Davidson's next game, to continue his scoring spree. The performance put him in the exclusive club of players who scored 30 points or more in their first four NCAA Tournament games. That club includes three-time NBA champion Clyde Lovellette, former ABA and NBA player Jerry Chambers, and former NCAA Player of the Year Glenn "Big Dog" Robinson. Despite Stephen's impressive showing, Davidson lost to the eventual national champions, Kansas Jayhawks, 59-57, in a game that saw the youngster break the record for most three point shots made in a season.

Despite coming up short in the NCAA Tournament, this string of performances solidified Stephen's reputation as perhaps the best scorer in college, with an average of 32 points per game in those 4 tournament games. For his efforts, Stephen won Most Outstanding Player of the Midwest Region and was nominated for the ESPYs award for Breakthrough Player of the Year.

In Stephen's junior year, Davidson University's schedule got a lot tougher, but Stephen and his teammates were up for the challenge. Building on his impressive NCAA Tournament performance from the year before, Stephen became Davidson's all-time leading scorer on February 28th, 2009. He also helped Davidson achieve a 26-6 record again, and the team won the Southern Conference championship for the fourth consecutive year. However, they lost in the Southern Tournament semifinals, which put Davidson's bid to return to the NCAA Tournament in jeopardy.

In the end, Davidson wasn't given an invite to the NCAA Tournament, and it was a disappointment for the Davidson fan base. Stephen also had a disappointing game against the Loyola (Maryland) Greyhounds. Borrowing from their moniker, the Greyhounds hounded Stephen all throughout the game. They put at least two players on the standout, even if

Stephen didn't have possession of the ball. He was only able to hoist three shots, of which he missed. In the end, Stephen went scoreless for the first time in a long time.

But that didn't deter him. Instead of pouting, getting mad, or forcing his way to score, Curry helped the team by acting as a decoy. He set himself up in the corner - bringing two defenders with him. This gave the rest of the team a 4-on-3 advantage. By simply standing in the corner, he allowed his teammates to play inside, drive to the hoop, and eventually win over the Greyhounds by a whopping 30 points.

After being completely shut out for one game, Curry proved he was still a dangerous scorer, as he dropped 44 points in Davidson's next game against Oklahoma. He ended the season as the NCAA's scoring leader, with an average of 28.6 points per game, and was named an NCAA first-team All-American, as well as a John Wooden All-American.

By the end of the season, Stephen declared that he would enter the 2009 NBA Draft, foregoing his senior season of eligibility to get into the National Basketball Association and follow the path of his father. Upon his declaration, many highly respected scouts believed that he would be a sure-fire lottery pick and was ripe to begin producing immediately in the NBA.

Chapter 4:

Professional Life

Stephen Curry was considered one of the best prospects in the 2009 NBA Draft. In a draft class that included future All-Stars Blake Griffin, James Harden, and DeMar DeRozan, that's already quite a feat for someone yet to officially play on an NBA court. After all, it's rare to see someone who has legitimate point guard skills and can score from just about anywhere on the court.

However, just like earlier in his basketball journey, Stephen's lack of athleticism and size were still seen as major concerns. Still, many predicted that he was going to be at least a top 10 pick. Right before the draft, rumors were rife that the New York Knicks were intent on taking Stephen with their eighth pick, but another team beat them to the draw. The passionate fans of the Knicks were devastated when they heard Stephen's name before it was their team's turn to pick. It was the Golden State Warriors that chose Stephen's services, using the seventh overall selection to draft him. Almost immediately, he signed a 4-year rookie contract that was worth more than $12 million.

Right away, the Warriors found Stephen to be a reliable player, and he became an instant starter and contributor for the team. He had quite a number of highlights in his rookie year, contributing a number of 30 point games, 10 assist games, and even a triple-double. In fact, Stephen would end the season having the third-most 30 point, 10 assist games with five, only behind established superstars LeBron James and Dwyane Wade.

Because of his extraordinary performances, Stephen received an invite to the NBA All-Star Rookie-Sophomore Challenge, where he scored 14 points to help the Rookie team win. He also participated in the 3-Point Shootout, where he reached the final round before losing to veteran

Paul Pierce. After the All-Star break, Stephen continued his impressive season, becoming a serious contender for the Rookie of the Year award. He ended his rookie campaign with per-game averages of 17.5 points, 4.5 rebounds, 5.9 assists, and 1.9 steals. In addition to that, he nailed 166 3-pointers while shooting .437 percent from that range. Stephen finished second in the Rookie of the Year race to Tyreke Evans of the Sacramento Kings, but was unanimously named a member of the All-Rookie First Team.

After such a promising rookie season, Stephen picked up right where he left off for his 2010-2011 NBA season. Emerging as one of the best young point guards in the game, Stephen posted per-game averages of 18.6 points, 3.9 rebounds, 5.8 assists, 1.5 steals, and a very impressive .442 3-point shooting percentage. In addition to this, he also led the NBA in free throw percentage at 93.4%, which actually became the new Warriors record for single-season free throw accuracy. He won the 2011 NBA All-Star Skills Challenge, completing the obstacle course in 28.2 seconds in the final round.

Just when most people thought Stephen was ready to take the next step in his development, the injury bug hit him hard during the 2011-

2012 season. In the previous season, Stephen suffered a number of right ankle injuries. It was revealed that he had suffered ligament damage in that ankle, and that it would require surgery to repair the damage. He was ready by the end of the season, but he ran into a string of bad luck, spraining his surgically repaired ankle a number of times, including during the preseason.

Due to these injuries, he sustained even more damage to the ankle and was only able to play 26 of the possible 66 games, causing him to finish with a season-ending surgery on that same ankle. His averages went down to 14.7 points, 3.4 rebounds, 5.3 assists, and 1.5 steals in a disappointing campaign.

At the start of the 2012-2013 season, there were worries that Stephen had become injury-prone and that his ankle might prevent him from ever reaching his full potential. Despite this very real possibility, the Warriors showed full faith that he would wholly recover, giving him a 4-year contract extension worth $44 million. Stephen rewarded their faith by returning at the start of the season in great shape.

During the first three months of the season, it became evident that Stephen was making that jump from promising player to a full-time star. During that period, he averaged over 20 points and 6 assists per game, serving as the catalyst for the up-tempo style that the Warriors loved to play with, under Coach Mark Jackson. In February, Stephen stepped up his game even further, averaging 25 points and 7 assists per contest during the month.

One highlight in that month was a 54-point performance against the New York Knicks, the third-biggest scoring explosion seen at the world famous Madison Square Garden. By the end of the season, Curry had made a total of 272 3-pointers, breaking Ray Allen's previous record of 269 for the most 3-pointers made in a regular season. To add even more drama, Stephen wasn't able to set the record until the final day of the season! More importantly though, he led the Warriors back into the NBA Playoffs, where they hadn't been in more than five years.

In the Playoffs, not much was expected from the young Warriors squad. After all, while they were talented, they were also very young, and most of their players, including Stephen, were making their first playoff appearance. However, they immediately made noise as a sixth seed, eliminating the heavily favored Denver Nuggets, 4-2, behind a high-octane offensive barrage led by Stephen and his backcourt mate, Klay Thompson.

In the next round, they faced the San Antonio Spurs, one of the premiere franchises in the NBA. While the Warriors lost to the Spurs, led by the legendary Tim Duncan, the team went down with a tough fight. This playoff appearance served notice that Stephen Curry and the Warriors were looking to be tough customers in the coming years.

The 2013-14 NBA season saw Stephen achieve All-Star and All-NBA status. The fan-favorite was voted in as a Western Conference starter, while also being named to the All-NBA Second Team. Aside from his individual achievements, he helped Golden State improve to a 51-31 record. The sixth-seeded Warriors faced the Los Angeles Clippers in the first round of the NBA Playoffs. When the smoke cleared, the Warriors were left in the dust, despite another brilliant performance by Stephen, which included seven three-pointers and 33 points in Game 4. After the season ended in disappointment, Stephen and the Warriors vowed to work on their individual and collective game in the off-season so they could come back stronger. And they did.

The team won 67 games to take the top seed in the entire league. This marked the first time the franchise had clinched the best record since 1976. They also bagged their first NBA championship in 40 years after battling it out with the LeBron James-led Cleveland Cavaliers.

Old-hand Andre Iguodala was instrumental in the Warriors championship run and was named the Finals MVP. The 2014-15 season was even more memorable for Stephen as he won the Most Valuable Player Award - making his mark as one of the truly elite players in the game. Stephen was named to his second All-Star selection, while his fellow "Splash Brother" Klay Thompson got in for the first time.

Stephen received the most online votes on his way to the Western Conference All-Star starting lineup. This accomplishment showed that not only was he becoming one of the best players in the league, but he was also becoming a fan-favorite. During the All-Star festivities, Stephen won the 3-Point Shootout by besting the likes of James "The Beard" Harden, Kyrie Irving, Marco Belinelli, and teammate Klay Thompson.

In the 2014-15 campaign, Stephen averaged 24 points, 4.3 rebounds and a career-high 8.5 assists in 78 games. Among the points he scored during the season was his 1,000th career three pointer which he made in his 369th game – the fastest by any player in NBA history. He also became the fastest player to hit 100 three pointers in NBA Playoff history, which he accomplished in just 28 games.

In the ongoing 2015-16 NBA season, Stephen has improved by leaps and bounds. In fact, there have been talks that Stephen is on cue to become the first ever winner of both the Most Valuable Player and Most Improved Player awards.

Stephen's mother, Sonya, may have played a big role in her son's ever-improving game. Mrs. Curry once stated in an interview with the *San Francisco Chronicle* that her son pays her $100 for every turnover he commits during a game. While $100 is pocket change to a multi-millionaire like Stephen, the basketball superstar does mind paying up. He sees every $100 dollars as equivalent to a turnover that may have dictated the flow of the game. Plus, he gets a good ribbing from Mom. Stephen relates that his mom likes to text him to remind him about the bet. She often says "some witty one-liner about what she's going to buy".

The "fine", which is held by a verbal contract between mother and son, helps Stephen focus on his game a little more. Stephen admits that the bet "keeps (him) on the edge every game." Sonya allows her son three errors each game but every turnover he makes after that will go to the pool which Sonya collects at the end of the season. Stephen says his wife, Ayesha, helps him choose what to buy his mother using the money he lost through the bet.

So far in the 2015-16 season, Stephen is averaging almost 34 points per game. That's a ten-point improvement from last year's MVP campaign. The "Baby-Faced Assassin" is also on track to improve his rebounds and steals average, along with his two-point and three-point field goal percentage, and free throw shooting. He just passed his father Dell on the NBA's list of career three-pointers made.

He has drilled 1,262 three point field goals so far and is on schedule to reach or break the 1,500 mark by season's end. Stephen is now number 36 on the all-time list, while semi-retired sharpshooter Ray Allen is still lording it over at number 1 with 2,973. Stephen can easily reach that number if he continues to play at this level (he's making 5 three pointers per game) for the next five years, give or take.

Stephen and the rest of "Dub Nation" is out to prove that they are no fluke, that their championship season was no one-time thing. The Golden State Warriors are as hungry as ever. Like its superstar franchise player, the Warriors have their doubters. Even after winning the 2014 NBA Championship, people still question the team's greatness.

No doubt, the diminutive Stephen has been trying to prove himself since he was a youngster. Now it's his team's turn to prove the naysayers wrong. Even with the Larry O'Brien Trophy in their trophy case and the championship rings on their fingers, they still play as if they're out for blood. They are out to build a legacy.

Stephen sums it all up in an interview with *USA Today*. Asked about his team's success (they are riding a 14-0 win-loss record as of this writing), Stephen simply said it's "because (they) want to be great." And from the looks of it, they're on their way.

As for his own career, he calls his journey from being a long shot to one of the most recognized faces in the world as the "ultimate paradox of a story". As we know, Stephen came out of high school with no outsiders believing he could become who he is today. Not one major college recruited him. He was deemed too small and too soft. But look at him now. He's the biggest topic in the NBA right now - thanks to his incredible work ethic, resiliency, attention to detail, and belief in himself.

Chapter 5:

Personal Adult Life

On the court, Stephen's game has obviously evolved. He's become a great facilitator, getting his big men involved in the offense, and he has been getting better at defense and limiting his turnovers every season.

Off the basketball court, Stephen hasn't really changed much at all. Just like when he was a kid, he calls Charlotte, North Carolina his home during the offseason. According to his sister, Stephen was a goofball as a kid. Even his high school coaches fell victim to his pranks. Stephen the adult is no different in this regard. His wife,

Ayesha, also relates how crazy and silly Stephen can get when they're at home. He still likes to crack jokes and act like a goofball while playing with his three-year old.

While his youthful looks dictate that he's still young, Stephen actually has a beautiful family of his own. On July 30th, 2011, he married his longtime girlfriend, Ayesha Alexander, in his hometown of Charlotte. They actually met each other in a church youth group when Stephen was just 15 years old. They had their first daughter, Riley, on July 19th, 2012. Ayesha gave birth to their second daughter, Ryan, on July 10th, 2015. Stephen's family is very important to him and he keeps his personal life as his highest priority. He is also known as a devout Christian, and he shows it on the court by writing various verses on his game shoes. One of his personal favorites is Philippians 4:13.

In addition to his burgeoning basketball skills, his marketability is also starting to go off the charts. In 2013, Stephen signed with the giant athletic wear company, Under Armour. With this contract, Stephen is expected to headline Under Armour endorsers in the NBA, which include the likes of Brandon Jennings and Kemba Walker.

Chapter 6:

Philanthropies and Charitable Acts

Stephen is also very active when it comes to community work; he is involved with a number of charities that help many people worldwide.

Stephen is an active supporter of the United Nations Foundation. The group is well-known for its different projects that help resolve world issues, such as: health, socioeconomic, environmental, and humanitarian challenges. This forward-thinking group is always on the lookout for plausible solutions to these problems, and is able to do so by promoting advocacies, performing various campaigns, and making strategic alliances with both public and private groups.

One project of the United Nations Foundation that Curry is actively involved in is the Nothing But Nets program. Inspired by sportswriter Rick Reilly, this project thrives through the work of thousands of individuals, with the most active participants being professional athletes. Stephen first became aware of the dangers of malaria after his friend and former college roommate Bryant Barr started Buzz Kill, a charitable three-on-three basketball tournament that was formed to help deal with the dreaded disease.

The Nothing But Nets project aims to provide bed nets in various locations in Africa, where malaria is considered to be one of the leading causes of death in children. His endeavor led him to Tanzania in 2013, where Stephen personally gave away mosquito nets that had been treated with insecticides. To date, Nothing But Nets has provided more than 9 million nets to people across Africa since 2006. On his part, Stephen has been responsible for around 38,000 nets. So the next time you cheer Stephen for a three-point shot he makes, remember that you're cheering for the people, especially the children, of Africa and other malaria-stricken parts of the world. Stephen has pledged three mosquito nets for every three pointer he makes. Talk about motivation.

But that's not his only contribution to the fight against malaria. Stephen has garnered the help of some of his fellow NBA stars who, like him, donate mosquito nets. He is also actively speaking about the issue any chance he gets. In fact, he held a post-game chalk talk with some fans early in 2015, during which he discussed malaria and its dangers.

Stephen's dedication to the fight against malaria has garnered the attention of the world and one particular head of state. He was invited to the White House by none other than the President of the United States. Like the basketball superstar, President Barack Obama is a staunch advocate for a malaria-free world. Stephen was asked to give a speech in front of numerous media personnel inside the Eisenhower Executive Office Building. After the talk, Stephen met with the President in the famed Oval Office and the two discussed the President's Malaria Initiative and the First Lady's "Let's Move" campaign. They also managed to talk some golf and basketball.

Stephen is also an active supporter of the Animal Rescue Foundation, or A.R.F. This group's main advocacy is for the needs of various companion animals, such as cats and dogs. Their main mode of action is to save animals that are abandoned at public shelters and then distribute them to a home where they will be loved and wanted. This group not only saves the lives of companion animals, but also makes the lives of both young and old humans much better.

Stephen has his own charity in the Stephen Curry Foundation. He is also closely tied to ThanksUSA, a public charity which helps provide scholarships for the spouses and children of those in active service in the U.S. military. He is, in fact, the national spokesperson for the charity since 2010. Also an avid golfer, Stephen has established an annual golf tournament in San Francisco that will benefit ThanksUSA.

The Babyfaced Assassin also holds basketball camps whenever he can. He hosts one with Klay Thompson, which they call Splash Brothers Basketball Clinic. Stephen likes to visit hospitals to cheer up some young patients whenever he can. He also helps out with the Feed the

Children program, which fed 400 families around the Bay Area. To give under-served young people an opportunity to experience the NBA in person, Stephen gives away 15 tickets for each home game.

Last but not least, Stephen is an active participant in the NBA Cares program, the charity arm of the National Basketball Association. Through NBA Cares, players, coaches, and other team officials get to help work on building their local communities. They perform numerous projects, including reading to the children, building homes for the less fortunate, and administering sports clinics in order for kids to get engaged in fitness, which includes hosting a Get Fit Hoops and Health Clinic that caters to more than 250 children.

To show gratitude for his seemingly endless desire to help others, Stephen was given the 2013-14 Kia Community Assist award. The award is given to an NBA player who best exemplifies the passion of the league to give back to the community. Stephen then forwarded the $25,000 reward money from the NBA and Kia to ThanksUSA, his chosen charitable institution.

Chapter 7:

Legacy, Future, and Inspiration

Currently, Stephen is seen as one of the best point guards in the National Basketball Association. Combining great court vision and feistiness with incredible shot-making ability, his game has captivated both purists and casual viewers.

He has managed to become one of the most dominant point guards in the game, which is no small feat, because today's NBA is littered with a multitude of superstar point guards such as

Russell Westbrook, Damian Lillard, Chris Paul, and John Wall. The point guard position right now is the most talented that it has ever been, which makes it an astounding accomplishment for Stephen to be right there among the top.

As he's yet to reach his prime, the ultimate legacy of Stephen Curry is still to be written. However, it's easy to see, for now, that his ultimate standing among the best players of the game will be dictated by how far he can take the Golden State Warriors. Buoyed by arguably the best fans in the NBA, the Warriors of today play a frenetic style of basketball that is predicated on speed and sharpshooting.

Because of his elite talents, Stephen is seen as a next-generation superstar in the NBA. He has quite a unique skill set: his ball-handling and passing abilities allow him to play like a true point guard should; his playmaking skills seem best-suited for the open court. However, his movement without the ball also allows him to hold his ground when the game is slowed down. Obviously, the one skill that gets the most attention is his scoring ability. Since high school, he's been known as a phenomenal scorer, with a quick release and almost-infinite range. It's his shooting that makes him such a tough cover for any team, but it's his attention to detail and improvement each and every year that allow him to stay ahead of the opponents' schemes.

Because he has such a unique skill set, it is tough to make an actual comparison for Stephen. His ability to balance creating shots for himself and others gets him compared to past and present "point gods" like Steve Nash and Tim Hardaway. For those who want to take it further, some even compare him to the all-timers Rick Barry and Jerry West. However, the player he is most compared to, due to his almost-perfect shooting stroke, is future Hall of Famer Ray Allen.

The forecast for Stephen's future is still up for debate. At the tender age of 27 years old, there are still a lot of things that can be accomplished by this guy. If his shooting pace continues, it is widely forecasted that within 10 years, there is the potential for him to go down as the greatest 3-point shooter the NBA has ever seen.

In his current pace, he's on track to eventually break Ray Allen's record for the most career 3-pointers, which currently stands at more than 2,800 (and counting, as Allen is still considered an active player). Other than the volume of 3-pointers he makes, Stephen's 3-point shooting percentage is also remarkable. His current career 3-point percentage (.446) is probably the highest percentage ever recorded for a player who shoots as many difficult shots as he does.

But other than his unique ability to shoot the rock, Stephen is also seen as a strong presence on his team. He possesses strong leadership traits, with the ability to rally teammates, both skilled and not-so-skilled, to keep playing at their best. Because of this characteristic, he is considered as an undisputed leader and franchise player of the Warriors, with his influence on the team going beyond the stat sheet.

Lastly, one of Stephen's underestimated characteristics is his competitive spirit. It may not show all the time, due to his stoic, baby-faced look during and especially after games, but Stephen is actually one of the most competitive players in the league. While he may not be too expressive on the court, he is the type of guy that has his motor running for the entire duration of the game. He's known for orchestrating come-from-behind wins and putting away opponents with dagger plays. Make no mistake about it, Stephen is a killer on the court.

For young ones everywhere, Stephen Curry seems to be the ideal guy to use as a basketball inspiration. His basketball skills are tailor-made for those who don't really have elite-level athleticism. His life story reflects an underdog who battled odds in order to become one of the best in his profession. In spite of his slight frame, he embodies the important values of leadership and toughness. Last but not least, his humility and heart, on and off the court, make him a great role model for serious basketball followers and casual fans alike.

Conclusion

I hope this book served its purpose in helping you gain inspiration from the life story of Stephen Curry, one of the best players currently playing in the National Basketball Association.

The rise and fall of a star is often the cause for much wonder, but most stars have an expiration date. In basketball, once a star player reaches his mid- to late-thirties, it is often time to contemplate retirement. What will be left in people's minds about that fading star? In Stephen Curry's case, people will remember how he led a franchise in their journey towards a championship, and possibly multiple championships. He will be remembered as the guy who plucked his franchise from obscurity, helped them build their image, and honed his own image along the way.

Stephen Curry wasn't always the first choice while growing up, or in the draft, for that matter. He didn't always succeed in his early years, and struggled to get noticed in his high school days. But as soon as he got his opportunities, he worked hard to maintain his standing and to reach the top.

Stephen has also inspired so many people because he is the star who never failed to look back. He's the one who paid his dues forward by helping thousands of less-fortunate youth find their inner light through sports - specifically basketball.

Another thing that stands out about Stephen's story is the fact that he never forgot where he came from. As soon as he had the capacity to give back, he poured what he had straight back to those who needed it, and he continues to do so to this day.

Now that you've learned some of the great lessons from Stephen's story, you can use them to uplift yourself and the lives of those around you. Good luck in your own journey!

26922515R10035

Made in the USA
Middletown, DE
08 December 2015